Ann Marie O'Neill

Popular
Quimper

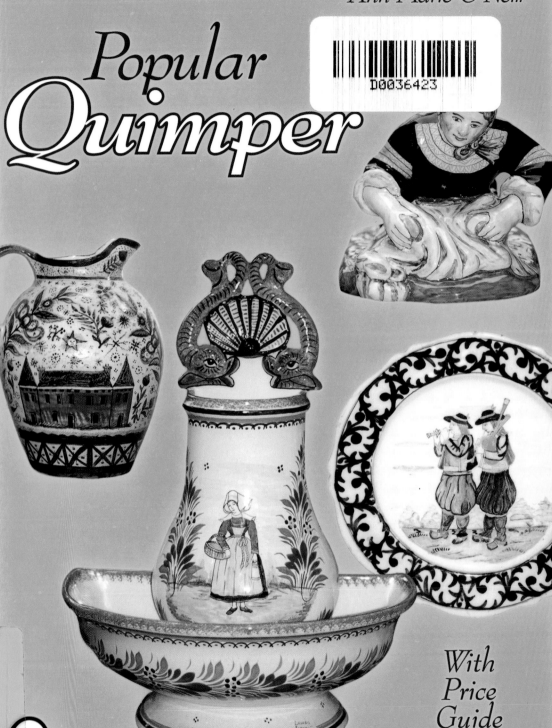

With
Price
Guide

A Schiffer Book for Collectors

About the Author

Although Ann Marie O'Neill has lived in New England her entire life, she is a born traveler. About twenty years ago, Ann Marie was introduced to French *faïence*, Quimper, and Malicorne, at *Marcia and Bea's* charming shop in Newton Highlands, Massachusetts, where she and her mother would admire and sometimes buy a piece of old Quimper. She is now a leading dealer, making regular pilgrimages to France in search of old Quimper ware, always scouring the markets in Paris, Brittany, and the south of France. The search for just the right piece of old *faïence* for both the beginning and advanced collector is always an exciting challenge.

Ann Marie exhibits at antique shows in New England, New York, Texas, and Florida, and leads a group of Quimper enthusiasts to France every year. A large mail order business, an occasional lecture about old Quimper, and private appointments contribute to a very busy schedule that still allows time for travel to Greece, Istanbul, and Italy, but most especially time for her three treasured grandchildren.

A graduate of Regis College in Weston, Massachusetts, Ann Marie taught elementary school for a number of years. She and her husband reside in Duxbury, Massachusetts, near the sea, and spend much of the winter skiing on the slopes of Loon Mountain near their home in North Woodstock, New Hampshire.

Popular Quimper

ANN MARIE O'NEILL

Dedication

Dedicated to all the dealers and collectors of Quimper *faïence,* who share in my love of fine French faïence.

Copyright © 2000 by Ann Marie O'Neill
Library of Congress Catalog Card Number: 99-69984

Designed by Bonnie M. Hensley
Type set in ZapfChan Bd BT/Korinna BT

ISBN: 0-7643-1099-2
Printed in China
1 2 3 4

Published by Schiffer Publishing Ltd.
4880 Lower Valley Road
Atglen, PA 19310
Phone: (610) 593-1777; Fax: (610) 593-2002
E-mail: Schifferbk@aol.com
Please visit our web site catalog at
www.schifferbooks.com

In Europe, Schiffer books are distributed by
Bushwood Books
6 Marksbury Avenue Kew Gardens
Surrey TW9 4JF England
Phone: 44 (0)208-392-8585;
Fax: 44 (0)208-392-9876
E-mail: Bushwd@aol.com
Free postage in the UK. Europe: air mail at cost.

This book may be purchased from the publisher.
Include $3.95 for shipping. Please try your bookstore first.
We are always looking for people to write books on new and related subjects.
If you have an idea for a book, please contact us at the address above.
You may write for a free catalog.

Contents

Introduction

Kwimper, Kwimpair, Kimper, or Kem - páir

Kemper, once a small village, was established by the Celts in the fifth century near the southern coast of Brittany. The Celts named the village *Kemper* (pronounced **KEM PAIR**). Today the people of Brittany proudly strive to preserve their Celtic heritage, especially their language, music, dance, traditional cooking, and pottery.

An Alfred Beau masterpiece. Looking up the Odet River to Quimper with the spires of the Cathedral in the background.

Quimper, now a city of more than 70,000 people, is located 350 miles west of Paris and is known as the city of flowers and art. The Odet River flows through the center of Quimper and past the *faïencerie* (pottery factory) that has been producing *faïence* (pottery) since 1690 when Jean Baptiste Bousquet built the first kilns. For many years, the pottery was loaded on to boats on the Odet River and shipped to other regions of France. Today, the *faïence* is packed and shipped by air, land, and sea to many places around the world.

The rooftops of Quimper, a large city.

Over the 300 plus years of pottery production, there have been three major and two minor factories in Quimper. The three major factories were the Grande Maison HB, Eloury-Porquier, and Henriot. Interestingly, all three larger factories were gradually merged into one and that one is now owned and operated by Americans under the name *Société Nouvelle des Faïenceries de Quimper.* One of the two smaller factories, Keraluc, was purchased by the American group in 1990, while the other, the Fouillen faïencerie, under the direction of Maurice Fouillen, is still located near the *rue Jean Baptiste Bousquet* in Quimper.

Pricing

Pricing in this book is strictly a guide. Prices of many antiques are increasing all the time, and at different rates depending on many factors: supply and demand, rarity, condition, and, in the case of Quimper, the value of the US dollar against the French franc. It is very important to note that prices vary for a number of reasons. In different parts of the United States, prices also vary due to supply and demand. If Quimper ware is seldom available in an area, prices for what is available will be higher than in an area where Quimper ware is more plentiful. Wares that are in short supply everywhere, such as the wares of Alfred

Beau, are always expensive and always increasing in value. Unique and unusual pieces are also ever increasing in price.

Of course, the condition of a piece also affects its value. A large and/or new chip or crack will reduce the value of a piece by at least one-half. Tiny glaze flakes, rim wear, and general signs of wear shouldn't affect value at all. (After all, we are talking about something that is at least fifty years old.) Small and unobtrusive old chips, that are dark in color, have only a slight, if any affect on price. These minor flaws should not be restored. Professional restoration usually does not affect value, but should be noted, because restored pieces should not be immersed in water. If a piece is not marked and you aren't sure if it is authentic, don't buy it without the advice of a very knowledgeable dealer.

At the start of the twenty-first century, pieces of Quimper are becoming less and less available on the market. As a result prices are increasing at a rapid rate and inflation should be taken into consideration when regarding the prices herein. (As of January 2000, a recommended 10% should be added to all prices.)

The center of old Quimper.

Chapter One
The Grande Maison HB

In 1690, Jean-Baptiste Bousquet established what was to become the first important pottery of modern times on the banks of the Odet River in Locmaria, a tiny hamlet on the outskirts of Quimper. The location was ideal as there were natural clay deposits in the area, nearby forests to supply the fuel needed for the ovens, and the river could be used for shipping.

A street, located adjacent to the *Musée de la Faïencerie* in Quimper, named after the founder of the *Grande Maison HB*.

In the eighteenth century, the factory that became known as the *Grande Maison* expanded and flourished, producing everyday tablewares and pipes. Late in the nineteenth century, as the railroads began to criss-cross France, tourists from Paris and all of France flocked to the seaside villages of Brittany for their *vacances*. By this time the theme known as "the *petit Breton*" had emerged and its appearance on the *faïence* of Quimper reflected the simple life of Brittany's peasants. Wares were decorated with country folk (the *Petit Breton*), sometimes rendered in a simple, almost crude style and sometimes in a naive, yet detailed manner. What better memento of a sojourn in the country than a sweet piece of *faïence* decorated in the sunny colors of summer, featuring endearing peasant figures in their local costumes?

The perfect souvenir. A pair of early mugs. 3" tall. Unsigned. c. 1890. $150-175 ea.

The first mark to be used by the *Grande Maison* appeared about 1860 and was not registered until 1882.

First HB mark. Wares from the *Grande Maison* were first marked with "HB" from 1860 to 1883, registered in 1882.

From 1883 to approximately 1904 another variation of the "HB" was used.

Second HB mark.
1880s to 1895.

As is often said "imitation is the sincerest form of flattery." Late in the nineteenth century, the competing *faïencerie* in nearby Malicorne noted the success of the *faïence* from Quimper and began to produce copies of this popular folk art (see page 147, Chapter Eight). As a result the *faïenceries* in Quimper, especially the Porquier factory, often added the identifying word "Quimper" to their wares beginning late in the nineteenth century (no specific date is known).

HB Quimper mark with tiny symbols to identify the artist, used until 1942. Also used with initials from 1942 to 1968. Again used with the letters "f" (with a number for form) and "d" (with a number for decoration) from 1968 to 1983. These are important distinctions when dating a piece.

The early years of the twentieth century were difficult years for the *Grande Maison*. The factory was in dire need of modernization and cash flow was tight. In fact, during World War I, the *Grande Maison* employed only about three workers. Fortunately, in 1917, Jules Verlingue, a potter from Boulogne-sur-Mer, in northern France, purchased the *Grande Maison* and set about rejuvenating it.

In 1918, Jules moved the *Grande Maison* to a new and modern facility on the *rue Haute* in Quimper. At about the same time, new *décors* were created and new artists were hired. Paul Fouillen, who joined the *Grande Maison* in 1920, introduced a new, modern Art Deco look to the *faïence*; however, he left the *Grande Maison* in 1929 to open his own *faïencerie* just around the corner from the HB factory. Fouillen's work was very popular and continues to be so today.

Fortunately, I was able to photograph some of Fouillen's work produced in his own factory at a recent exhibit in Quimper. You will find those photographs later in the book. Following is a sample of the mark used by Fouillen in his own factory. Wares produced in the HB factory are signed "HB Quimper PFouillen."

Mark used by Paul Fouillen for wares made in his own *faïencerie* after 1929.

Another landmark of the 1920s was the introduction of the Odetta line. Similar to *grès* (stoneware), the Odetta line featured bold shapes and colors with angular lines. Odetta was a huge success; it continues to be in great demand today. Each piece in the Odetta line was marked "HB Quimper Odetta" and production of Odetta continued until 1960.

HB Odetta mark. Used from 1922 to 1960.

Sadly, World War II intervened. While production was very limited during the war years, modernization followed in the post war years, and, as a result, the finished product acquired a noticeably new look—a look that was polished and more perfect. Fortunately, the tradition of hand painting continued and is still being done today.

Jean-Yves Verlingue succeeded his father, Jules, as the owner of the HB factory. After a recession in 1968 forced the Henriot factory (one of the other two major *faïenceries* in Quimper) to close, Jean-Yves purchased all of Henriot's assets (which, we will see later, included all the marks, molds, and patterns of the Porquier factory, the third major factory). At this point, all three major *faïenceries* were one. Business remained steady until 1983 when labor problems plagued the factory and foreign competition caused a sharp drop in sales. Bankruptcy was declared.

In 1984, the *Société Nouvelle des Faïenceries de Quimper*, a company formed by a group of Americans and headed by Sarah and Paul Janssens, was selected by French authorities to rescue the HB-Henriot *faïencerie*. Today, the factory is thriving, employing 131 people in 1999.

The mark currently in use by the *Société Nouvelle des Faïenceries de Quimper.*

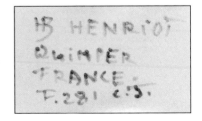

This is a small sampling of wares from the *Grande Maison*. You will find more HB wares later in the book.

A tall salt glazed jug from the *Grande Maison HB*. Value not available. About 14" tall. *Courtesy Musée de la Faïence Quimper.*

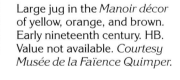

Large jug in the *Manoir décor* of yellow, orange, and brown. Early nineteenth century. HB. Value not available. *Courtesy Musée de la Faïence Quimper.*

The *décor* on this bowl is almost too charming to fill it with strawberries and cream. About 10" long, 8" wide. "HB Quimper." c.1930. $300-325.

A lovely pair of plates in the HB *croisillé décor*. These floral sprays and this criss-cross pattern will always distinguish wares from the HB factory. 9.5" dia. "HB Quimper." c.1925. $350-375 ea.

A large tray featuring a pair of musicians who seem to be enthralled in their music. Again the criss-cross pattern and floral sprays immediately identify this as a piece from the HB factory. 13.5" x 16.5". "HB Quimper." c. 1935. $750-800.

An interesting pair of vases with very unusual topiaries to either side of the *Breton* figures. Wonderful shades of green used here. Graceful handles sponged in blue. About 10" tall. "HR Quimper." c. 1910. $1,200-1,300 pr.

An exquisite pair of vases in the Rococo style. Bordered with yellow and blue scrolls in relief. Raised detail on the sides as well. Nicely rendered *Breton* couple. 6" tall. "HB Quimper." c.1910. $1100-1200.

This bust of a *Breton* fisherman is a pepper shaker; a mate for salt also exists. 3" tall. c.1925. $175-200.

Simple, elegant *décor*. A sweet sabot decorated with a blue *fleur de lis* and poised on a rectangular base decorated with black ermine tails and blue dot *décor*. Base is 2.25" x 3.5", 3.5" tall. "HB Quimper." c.1910. $225-250.

Chapter Two
Eloury Porquier

Francois Eloury, a former employee of the *Grande Maison*, established a second factory in Locmaria in 1779. By the middle of the nineteenth century, the Eloury factory was flourishing. In 1869, Augustine Porquier, wife of Adolphe Eloury, a descendant of Francois Eloury, assumed the position of director of the *faïencerie*. Then, in 1872, Madame Porquier hired the artist Alfred Beau, and thus began the Golden Age of the *faïence* of Quimper.

While Beau lacked formal training, his artistic genius was immediately evident in his work. The quality of his artistry is unequaled in the three hundred years of *faïence* production in Quimper. As you would expect, Beau's work is vigorously sought after by collectors in France, the US, England, Belgium, and many other countries.

The first series Alfred Beau created for Madame Porquier was the *Botanique* series. The series consists of more than 100 *poncifs* (patterns), featuring exquisite florals accented with insects, birds, and sea life. For his second series, *Scenes Bretonne*, Beau sketched and painted over 200 endearing scenes of bucolic life in Brittany. Each scene elicits a vignette in the imagination of the beholder. His third series, *Legendes Bretonnes,* depicts famous *Breton* legends.

In addition to plates and pitchers, Beau molded complex forms such as musical instruments, mirrors, clocks, vases, inkwells, et cetera, and lavished them with his botanicals and scenes. Most are signed with one of two marks used by the Porquier factory. One was first used about 1875 and the other about 1894. Both marks are referred to as first period Porquier marks: 1875-1903.

First "PB" mark to be used.
First period: 1875-1903.

Another "PB" mark to be used.
First period: 1894-1903.

The PB mark on the wares in the *Scenes Bretonnes* series was often accompanied by the name of the town where the scene was set, including Quimper. However, as noted above, there is evidence that about 1895 the word "Quimper" was occasionally added to wares from the PB factory, mainly to distinguish them from copies being produced in Malicorne and Desvres. As a result, contrary to an earlier opinion, the mark "PB Quimper" can be found on a first period piece of any type from 1895 to 1903 (the years of the first period), including botanicals and scenes not set in Quimper. Previously, it was believed that "Quimper" was added to the marks in 1904, exactly.

"PB" with the name of the town where the scene is set—
Rosporden and the word Quimper (used to insure its authenticity as a product of the Porquier factory). 1894 -1903.

A second mark, "AP," was also used by the Porquier factory from approximately 1875 to 1905.

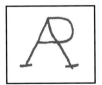

AP mark. 1875-1903. (Many
AP wares went unmarked.)

Despite the popularity of Beau's work and because of the copies being produced in Malicorne and Desvres, the Porquier factory experienced financial problems in the early 1890s. Sadly, Beau left in 1894. After Beau's departure, Adolphe's son Alfred continued production using an "AP" mark that Adolphe had registered earlier. However, many wares from 1895 to 1903 were not marked at all. In 1903, production was limited and then ceased altogether.

The following are examples of Porquier wares.

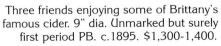

Three friends enjoying some of Brittany's
famous cider. 9" dia. Unmarked but surely
first period PB. c.1895. $1,300-1,400.

A very dear scene, banded in blue on blue *décor riche*, of a young *Breton* family. Crest of Brittany tops this wonderful 9" plate. "PB *Paludières de Saille*." c. 1880. $1,400-1,500.

Bell from the Porquier factory in the Delft *décor*. 6" tall. "PB." c. 1895. $550-600.

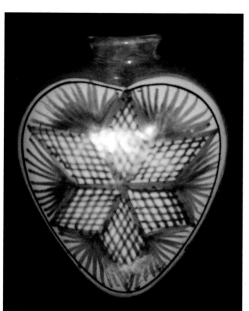

The Porquier factory produced many snuffs, which were often unsigned because of lack of space. The geometric *décor* on this sweet heart-shaped snuff is typical Porquier *décor*. About 2.5" tall. c. 1900. $525-550.

A *Breton*.

Crescent-shaped double inkwell rimmed in green acanthus *décor* and graced with a beautifully rendered young *Breton* couple. 7.5" long." "PB." c.1890. $1,600-1,800.

An exquisite pedestal base bowl with a scalloped rim banded in yellow. Spectacular botanical. c.1885. $3,800. *Courtesy Musée de la Faïence Quimper.*

Bonbonière in the soft pale blue glaze typical of first period PB wares, decorated with a lovely floral spray and a tiny butterfly. "PB." c.1885. $3,400. *Courtesy Musée de la Faïence Quimper.*

Three generations are gathered round the table on this large crescent vase. The elder *Breton* is most assuredly giving advice to the younger gentleman. An Alfred Beau masterpiece. 10" tall, 14" wide. "PB Rosporden Quimper." c.1885. $3,000-3,200.

The reverse of the vase (seen above).

The artistry of Alfred Beau is evident in the faces of this demure, sweet, young *Breton* couple. "PB." c.1885. Value not available. *Courtesy Musée de la Faïence Quimper.*

Plaque de proprêté or door plate featuring a portly *Breton* enjoying his pipe. 9.75" tall, 3.25" wide. "PB." c.1890. $925-950.

A tall ewer featuring two children with a little wooden boat! The handle and the face on the end of the piece illustrate Beau's creative talent. "PB." c.1885. Value not available. *Courtesy Musée de la Faïence Quimper.*

Decorative plaque in relief. The Odet River looking toward Quimper on a slightly misty day. The dark smoke on the right bank could be coming from one of Quimper's *faïenceries*. 15" tall, 18" long. "PB." c.1885. Value not available. *Courtesy Musée de la Faïence Quimper.*

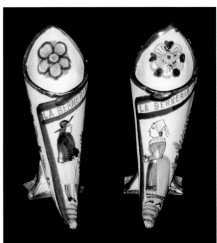

A sweet pair of *porte-bouquets* with classic AP figures. 4" tall. Unmarked but surely AP. c.1910. $550-575 pr.

A view looking up the Odet River toward the center of Quimper.

A close look at the scene on a platter by Alfred Beau. A masterpiece. 18" x 24". c.1885. Value not available. *Courtesy Musée de la Faïence.*

A *soupière* (without lid) with *touche décor* banded in blue and black. 6" dia. Unsigned AP. c.1880. $225-250.

Chapter Three
Henriot

Guillaume Dumaine established a factory in Locmaria on the outskirts of Quimper in 1789. Production was limited to *grès* ware (stoneware), until the mid nineteenth century when the factory expanded to include the production of *faïence*. Jules Henriot, a descendant of Dumaine, assumed the position of director of the *faïencerie* in 1884. Jules was only eighteen at the time.

The first mark to be used by the Henriot factory was "HR." This mark first appeared on the wares in 1891 but was not registered until 1904.

The first "HR" mark of the Henriot factory,
used from 1891 to 1895, registered in 1904.

The "HR" mark with the addition of the
word "Quimper" (approx. 1904).

Young Jules was an astute businessman. While he was busy expanding and modernizing the factory, trains were reaching out from Paris all across France. The trains brought tourists to Brittany's small villages and to the spectacular *Breton* coast. In addition, the people of Brittany, anxious to preserve their heritage, set their tables and decorated their homes with the wares from Quimper that reflected their traditions. Young Jules expanded his business to meet the increasing demands of the rapidly growing domestic and tourist markets. A gaily decorated piece of *faïence* was the perfect memento of a sojourn to Brittany, and this is still very true today.

In 1913, Jules Henriot purchased the molds, *aquarelles* (water colors), *poncifs* (patterns), and marks of the then defunct Porquier factory. The magnificent wares created by Alfred Beau would not be lost over time and re-issues would now be possible. Beginning in 1919, the Henriot *faïencerie* did reissue some of Alfred Beau's exquisite wares, marking them "PB Quimper" in order to distinguish them from the earlier production. The wares marked "PB Quimper" are known as second period Porquier Beau wares. As previously noted, some first period Porquier Beau pieces were also marked "PB Quimper." When a piece is marked "PB Quimper," one must use their visual and tactile skills to recognize the difference between first period (1875-1903) and second period (c.1919-1930) wares. However, because first period wares have a glaze that is bluish in tone and were painted with great attention to detail in soft, gentle tones, the difference can be easily detected.

The mark used by the Henriot factory when they re-issued Alfred Beau's work beginning in 1919.

After World War I, Jules hired Victor Lucas as technical director for the Henriot factory. Lucas introduced a new glazing process and led the factory into the Modern Movement period characterized by bold colors and new *décors*.

In 1922, a lawsuit that had been filed in 1898 by the *Grande Maison* was finally resolved ruling that the "HR" mark was altogether too similar to the *Grande Maison*'s "HB" mark. The court agreed with the *Grande Maison* and ordered the Henriot factory to change their mark. Henriot, the family name, was the logical choice for the new signature. By capitalizing the "H" and the "R" in Henriot, the new mark, "HenRiot," was reminiscent of their original "HR."

The Henriot mark introduced in 1922 and used until 1968. Used with a number, or with two or three little xxx and — (dashes) from 1922 to 1942, with initials 1942 to 1968, and with F (form) and D (*décor*) with numerals from 1968 to 1983. Remember all dates are estimations.

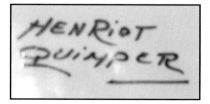

Following a devastating fire in 1925, young Jules again modernized and expanded the factory on a new site. Production continued to increase and the factory flourished. Probably the most prolific period for the Henriot *faïencerie* was the period between the two world wars. Traditional table wares, new molds, *décors*, and a myriad of figures and special editions were produced. Unfortunately, as one might expect, World War II had a huge effect on the *faïencerie*. Production decreased dramatically and much of what was produced was for the occupying German army. These pieces are often marked on the bottom with a swastika.

A period of rebuilding at the Henriot factory followed World War II and slowly the work force increased to two hundred. Unfortunately a recession in the 1960s led to the demise of the Henriot factory and bankruptcy was declared in 1968.

Jean-Yves Verlingue, owner of the *Grande Maison*, purchased the Henriot factory in 1968 and moved the workers and equipment into his factory. No one was laid off and all three of Quimper's *faïenceries* were now one.

Two adorable little plates for a doll's tea party. 2.25" dia. "HR Quimper." c.1910. $70-80 ea.

The *demi-fantaisie décor* on this bagpipe vase is enhanced with a soft blue ribbon, scallop and dash border, and four blue dot *décor*. The piper is clad in puffy yellow pants and a blue vest. 4.5" tall, 5" wide. "HR Quimper." c.1910. $450-500.

Another bagpipe vase but from a later period. Note the absence of detail as seen in the previous piece. However, the colors are vivid and the *biniou* player is rendered with some detail. Lovely raised stylized leaves on the right side. About 4" tall, 4" wide. "Henriot Quimper." c.1935. $350-375.

This lovely pair of vases, produced between the two world wars, is generously painted in the *demifantaisie décor*. One features a young man in gold puffy pants and the other a lady with a distaff. 9" tall. "Henriot Quimper." c.1925. $1,200-1,300 pr.

In the foreground is a sweet covered jam pot or *bonbonière*. Very delicate *décor*. Underplate is 6.5" dia. "HB Quimper." c.1910. $375-400.

A peasant lady framed by the two handles sponged in a gentle blue. A band of delicate touche florals with blue dot blossoms wraps around the bulbous base. 6" tall. "Henriot Quimper." c.1930. $400-425.

A sweet and finely rendered *Bretonne* adorns this lovely *jardinière*. The serpent-like handles are wonderful. 11" long, 6" tall. "Henriot Quimper." c. 1925. $650-675.

An exquisite bowl with a deeply scalloped rim banded in blue and gold with a charming blue chain. A young maiden with a water jug on her head is featured. 8.5". "Henriot Quimper." c. 1930. $450-475.

Chapter Four
The Marks

Dating a piece of Quimper ware would be simple if we knew exactly when a mark was first used, when it was changed, and when its use was discontinued. Unfortunately, there are only a couple of dates that are known to be exact. Most dates given here are approximations. There are always some pieces that slip out of the factory with no mark at all. While experience is the best teacher when it comes to identifying Quimper ware, I hope the photographs in this book familiarize you with the typical styles of each factory.

Grande Maison HB

1 - HB w/ tail	1860-1883
2 - HB w/ no tail	1883-1895
3 - HB Quimper	1895-1940s
4 - HB Quimper Odetta	1922-1960
5 - Fish (rare)	1924
6 - HB Quimper w/....—	to 1942
7 - HB Quimper w/ initials of artist	1942-1968
8 - HB Quimper in semi-circle w/ F & D	1968-1983
9 - HB Henriot Quimper	1984-present

1

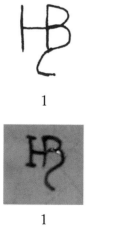

1

2

2

3

3

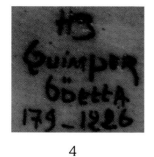

4

5

5

6 (with ....—)

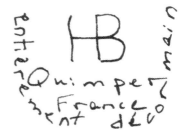

8

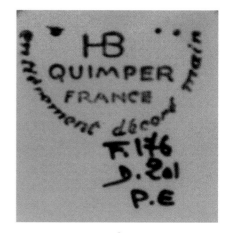

8

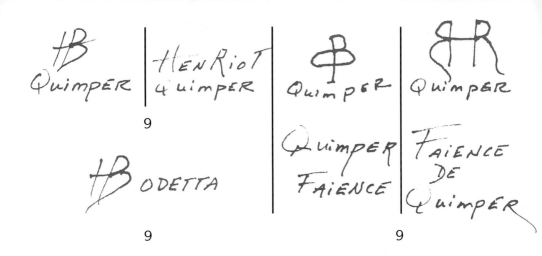

9

9   9

9

Porquier

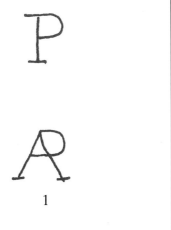

1

1

1

2

3

4

Henriot

1 - HR	1891-1895
2 - HR Quimper	1895-1922
3 - HenRiot Quimper	1922-1968
4 - Henriot Quimper	1922-1968
5 - PB Quimper	1919-1930
6 - Henriot Quimper in semi-circle w/ F & D	1968-1983
7 - HB Henriot Quimper	1984-present

1

1

5

5

2

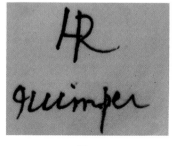

2

HR
Quimper
17

2

HenRiot
Quimper

3

HEnRiot
2 uimPER

FRANCE
76

3

HenRiot
QuimPER

3

HENRioT
QuimPER
159

3

HENRIOT
Quimper
France
entièrement décoré main

6

HB Henriot

7

Chapter Five
The *Petit Breton* and *Breton* Traditions

Sometime between the years 1860 and 1880 the *Petit Breton* theme crystallized. An unidentified artist employed by one of Quimper's three factories must have created the little peasant figures that have come to symbolize the *faïence* of Quimper, but which factory, no one can be certain. A *Breton*, a man, traditionally wears the puffy pants called *bragou-braz*, holds a cane or whip, and usually faces to the right. The *Bretonne*, a woman, also clad in the traditional style, usually holds a flower and faces to the left.

An unsigned and very primitive example of the "*Petit Breton*." A classic. 9" dia. c.1880. $275-300.

A pair of early plates in the primitive style. Note that the lady on this plate is almost identical with the lady in the photo on the previous page. 9" dia. c.1880. $550-600 pr.

This example has more detail than the two previous examples. Vivid color. 9" dia. c.1880. $325-350.

An oval plate marked only "HB." Soft blue, orange, and yellow *décor* surround this primitive *Breton*. 11" x 7.5". c.1890. $425-450.

In the *Breton* tradition, during the summer months, many towns hold a *Fest Noz,* or night festival, featuring *Breton* music and dance. During these festivals lots of crêpes and cider are consumed. These *Breton* traditons are evident in the wares produced in Quimper's *faïenceries. Biniou* (bagpipe) and *bombarde* (horn) players as well as dancers appear on a wide variety of wares.

These three young people are surely enjoying themselves as they dance the Celtic dance "*La Gavotte.*" Molded by Jim Sevellec for the Henriot factory. Details not available. *Courtesy Musée de la Faïence Quimper.*

Musical instruments were also produced but are extremely rare. However, many, many pieces were molded in the bagpipe shape.

Blue on blue *décor riche* border frames a pair of musicians on this simple, but lovely 9.5" plate. "Henriot Quimper." c.1935. $350-375.

Another pair of musicians are featured on this platter produced in the *Grande Maison*. This is the HB factory's version of the *croisillé* pattern. Small panels of blue and red criss-cross alternate with panels of flowers and four blue dot *décor* scattered about. 9.5" dia. "HB Quimper." c.1935. $425-450.

A spectacular tray featuring three
sweet young ladies in lovely dresses
enjoying the music of two musicians.
13.5" x 16.5". "HB Quimper." c.1910.
$1,200-1,300.

A Breton.

A young *Breton* sitting on a barrel playing his *bombarde* (horn.) He is clad in the traditional *bragou-braz* (puffy pants) and bright blue jacket. 14" tall. c.1920. "PB Quimper." $1,200-1,300.

The rich blue on blue *décor riche* frames a young and demure *Breton* couple. 11.5" long, 9" wide. "HR Quimper." c.1910. $450-475.

A vase for your flowers. A sweet rendition of a very popular form. 5.5" tall. "HR Quimper." c.1910. $550-575.

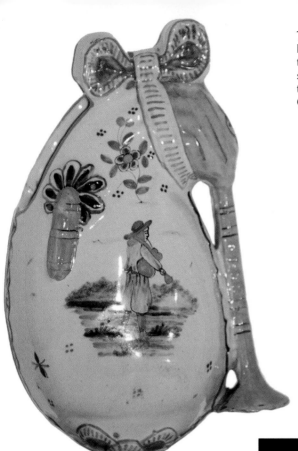

The *décor* is soft and sweet on this bagpipe made to be hung on the wall to hold flowers. This particular floral spray identifies this as a piece from the HB factory. 6" tall. "HB Quimper." c.1920. $375-400.

The Henriot factory produced this little bagpipe. Vivid color. 5" long. "HR Quimper." c.1915. $175-200.

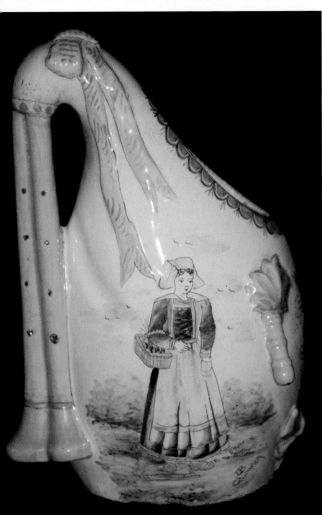

A demure *Bretonne* is featured on this exquisite example of a bagpipe. A tall vase decorated in soft pink, green, and blue, and accented with vivid yellow. 11" tall, 8" wide. "HB Quimper." c.1910. $850-900.

This bagpipe wall pocket is also from the *Grande Maison*. A *Bretonne* carries her basket and umbrella to market. 5.5" tall. "HB Quimper." c.1935. $175-200.

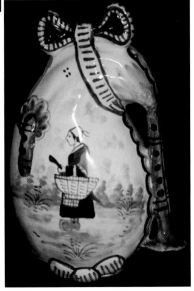

A wonderful pair of *biniou* shaped plates. The *Breton* figures and landscape are rendered in fine detail while the ribbons and floral sprays are exquisite. Approx. 9". "HB Quimper." c.1910. $850-900 pr.

Our two musicians in this instance lead a wedding procession. Note that these are the same musicians as on page 39. It was customary for artists to reuse one or more figures on any number of pieces. A collection of wares featuring the same figures would make an interesting collection.

Opposite page, bottom: A crescent or moon vase featuring both musicians and dancers. Second period Porquier Beau. 10" tall, 14" wide. "PB Quimper *Bannalec*." c.1920. $1,200-1,300.

This attractive dancing couple, rendered in fine detail, appears on a large plaque. Again you will see them on many different pieces. Note the lovely yellow and orange banding on the couple's costumes and their serene expressions.

Each year in July, a week-long Celtic festival is held in Quimper. This is the time for *Bretons* to celebrate their Celtic heritage.

Chapter Six
A Potpourri of Wares from Quimper

Flowers are a staple of life in Brittany. Homes are generously surrounded by lush gardens and fitted with window boxes laden with bright blossoms. Along the roadside, wildflowers of every color bloom. Town squares burst with color from their carefully tended gardens. It is no wonder that the wares of Quimper's *faïenceries* are lavishly decorated with flowers, both stylized and natural.

A *Breton* cottage in Quimper, "The City of Flowers and Art."

A spray of yellow *ajonc* often seen on the wares of Quimper.

A *Petit Breton* flanked by sprays of *ajonc*. Border of *ajonc* sprays and an interesting scallop and dot band. Unusual *décor*. 9.5" dia. "HB Quimper." c.1930. $375-400.

Flowers line the bridges across the Odet River in Quimper.

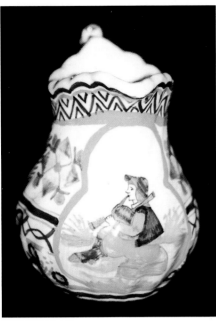

Stylized dogwood blossoms encircle this sweet little pitcher. Lavishly decorated. A *petit Breton* playing his bagpipe. Look for him on other Henriot pieces. 4" tall. "Henriot Quimper." c. 1930. $175-200.

À la touche décor of orange blossoms with green foliage and blue dot blossoms with yellow centers adorn this fantastic lavabo featuring a demure *Bretonne* on her way to market. The dolphin and scallop shell detail at the top of the fountain is spectacular. Base: 14" long x 8 3/4" wide, 6" tall. Top: 16" tall. "Henriot Quimper France." Price and date not avaliable.

Wonderful form and superb *décor* combine in this stunning vase. A charming young lady is flanked by tall floral sprays. Graceful handles are sponged in blue and the vase is outlined in a delicate blue scalloped line with small blue *touches*. This piece has it all! 9" tall. "HR Quimper." c. 1910. $650-700.

49

A tall, attractive two handled vase featuring our musicians. Sprays of *ajonc* and *bruyère* and green on green *décor riche* combine to frame the men. The reverse features the crest of Brittany. 15" tall. "HR Quimper." c.1915. $700-750.

An attractive vase in an old *décor* borrowed from a Marseille *faïencerie*. Early twentieth century "HB." Value not available. *Courtesy Musée de la Faïence Quimper.*

Normandie pattern vase featuring a lady clad in wooden shoes and the costume of Normandy. She carries a basket and an umbrella as she walks to market. Bold *décor riche* bands at the top and bottom frame the figure. One of *Les Provinces Francaise* series, which features peasants in the costumes of the different regions of France. 7.5" tall; base is 5" square. "HB Quimper." c.1940. $275-300.

Celtic bands encircle this vase featuring the two musicians. 10" tall. "HR Quimper." c.1915. $850-900.

Another *Breton* cottage.

Truly a fantastic piece. On her way home from the market this beautifully rendered *Bretonne,* clad in shades of pink and blue carries a basket of fish. Bold dragon handles are painted in fine detail. The blue on yellow *décor riche* on the sides is especially delicate and lovely. About 12" tall. "HR Quimper." c.1910. $2,000-2,200.

The other side of the vase features a fabulous spray of lilies.

An attractive *Breton* couple with sprays of *ajonc* and *bruyère,* and tasseled handles in yellow and blue. A charming pair of vases. 16" tall, 7.5" wide. "Henriot Quimper France." c.1925. $1,150-1,200.

The movement of the clouds and the billowing of the ladies' skirts give life to this vase by Jim Sévellec. A typical piece from the Modern Movement. Celtic bands encircle the vase. About 6" tall, 6" dia. "Henriot Quimper. " c.1930. $450-475.

A trumpet vase for your flowers. The *demi-fantaisie* floral sprays frame a charming *Bretonne*. 11" tall. "HR Quimper." c.1910. $600-650.

A fabulous pair of grandfather clocks. The *décor* is rendered in fine detail on these very important vases. Each features a finely rendered figure in a central medallion. 8" tall, 3" square. "Henriot Quimper France." c.1925. $1,500-1,600.

An attractive pair of vases: one features a *biniou* player, the other a *Bretonne* holding a distaff. Both figures are flanked with tall floral sprays. The scallop shell handles are a very popular accent on Quimper ware. 8" tall. "HR Quimper." c.1910. $825-850.

An attractive vase featuring a *Bretonne* flanked by large orange and blue blossoms. 9" tall, 5.25" across. "Henriot Quimper." c.1930. $375-400.

A demure young couple, perhaps courting, stand in front of a well. Bold blue on blue *décor riche* frames the front and back panels. An exquisite botanical on the back. 15" tall. "Henriot•Quimper France." c.1925. $1,050-1,100.

Spectacular fan shaped vase! The combination of the dolphin base, red and blue striped scallop shell above it, blue criss-cross, and scallop and dot *décor*, along with the beautifully rendered figures results in an exquisite piece. 8" tall, 10" wide. Unsigned but surely from Henriot. c. 1925. $625-650.

A young *Breton*.

An early three-fingered *tulipière* featuring a *Breton* couple picking apples. 7" tall, 7" wide. "HB." c. 1900. $575-625.

Opposite page, bottom: The central part of this very important piece is a vase in the crest form topped with a crown. The vase is flanked by the figures of a young, demure *Breton* couple. All three figures are mounted on an elaborate base. The imposing size (15" tall x 20" across) together with the three forms qualify this as a very important piece. "HR Quimper." c. 1910. $4,500-4,700.

57

The *Breton* scene on this *tulipière* is one of the loveliest I have seen, perhaps because the spires of the Cathedral in Quimper are such a strong symbol of Quimper for me. The spires can be seen from almost anywhere in the city. Here, a *Breton* peasant, sitting alongside the Odet River, with the spires of the Cathedral on the other side, plays his horn. Blue on yellow *décor riche* borders the base and sides. 7" tall, 6" wide. "HR Quimper." c. 1910. $700-750.

A simple *quintal* (five fingered vase) decorated with blue and orange *á la touche* blossoms. Simple but lovely. 5" tall. "Henriot Quimper." c. 1930. $175-200.

Another *tulipière* from the same *faïencerie,* but produced after 1922. The geometric details on this piece frame a nicely rendered *Bretonne* with her distaff. 7" tall, 5.25" wide. "Henriot Quimper." c. 1925. $500-525.

The *croisillé* pattern of the Henriot factory is one of the finest. Wares are lavishly decorated with blue criss-cross lines (known as *croisillé*), stylized flowers, blue dot *décor*, a variety of geometric accents, and nicely detailed *Breton* figures.

A wonderful example of Henriot's *croisillé* pattern. A portly *Breton* on his way to market with two baskets of fowl and a *Bretonne* fetching water adorn this lovely pair of plates. 10.5" dia. "Henriot Quimper France." c. 1930. $950-1,000 pr.

A covered dish with an attached underplate for your butter, jam, or bonbons. Generously decorated in the Henriot *croisillé* pattern. Lovely rippled form. About 6" dia. "Henriot Quimper." c. 1925. $425-450.

A sweet *Bretonne* resting with a basket of eggs at her side is featured on this pedestal base covered butter dish. About 6" dia. "Henriot Quimper." c.1930. $400-425.

Tea or coffee for two. An exquisite form—rippled and swirled. Sweet *décor*. Teapot is about 10" tall. "HR Quimper." c.1925. $800-850.

The *Ivoire Corbeille décor* comes in several varieties. Second-period Porquier Beau wares were made in the Henriot factory from about 1919. With some exposure to both first- and second-period wares, you will (in most cases, if not all) be able to identify the period correctly.

Three sweet pieces in the *Ivoire Corbeille décor*! Each piece is bright and sunny. The scallop shell: 8" dia., "Henriot Quimper France," c.1930, $225-250. The little pitcher: 4" tall, "*Auvergne Mont Doré,*" c.1930, $125-150. Covered, heart-shaped box: 6" dia., "Henriot Quimper," c.1930, $275-300.

An attractive crescent vase featuring a young man resting between chores. The scene is painted in fine detail. Blue on yellow *décor riche* bands on the sides. About 6" tall. "PB Quimper." c.1920. $900-950.

Scallop shell shaped bowl features a young mother adjusting her *coiffe* while a young girl holds a mirror for her. Blue on yellow *décor riche* border frames the scene. About 8" dia. "PB Quimper." c. 1920. $800-850.

Another crescent vase, but this one with stylized lizard handles. Two children with a pig. About 6" tall. "PB Quimper." c. 1920. $950-1,000.

The Odet River, which flows through the center of Quimper, is home to a few swans. They can often be seen in the spring gliding on the surface of the river with their young. Naturally, their graceful form interested the artists working in the *faïencerie* situated alongside the river.

A *petit cygne* (little swan) painted in soft blue and gold. The center panel features a horn player. Graceful form. 5" long, 4.5" tall. "HR Quimper." c.1910. $450-475.

A tiny swan tops a tobacco jar. Interesting shape. 4" tall. "Henriot Quimper." c.1930. $275-325.

A basket is formed by two swans, each with its neck arched up to form the handle. The basket is boldly decorated in cobalt blue and gold and features a *Bretonne* with her umbrella. A very popular form with collectors. 8.25" tall, 9" wide. "Henriot Quimper." c.1930. $575-600.

Same form as piece shown at bottom of previous page, but in a different palette. 9" tall, 9" wide. "Henriot Quimper." c.1930. $575-600.

A covered pot for your bonbons or perhaps for your trinkets! A pair of swans, again back to back with their necks forming the handle. *Ivoire Corbeille décor.* About 4" dia. "Henriot Quimper." c.1935. $275-300.

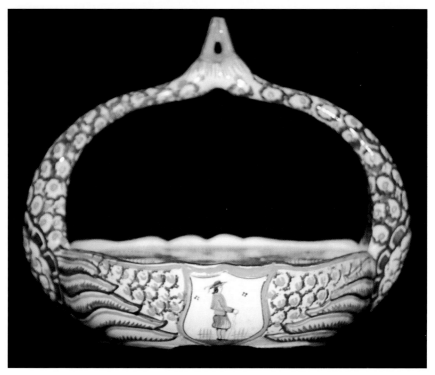

A very unusual form. Usually this form is an open basket, but this piece has depressions for eggs. 9.5" dia., 9.5" tall. "Henriot Quimper." c.1930. $850-900.

Swans have been molded in many forms over the years by the *faïenceries* in Quimper. This large *jardinière* is decorated in a rich cobalt blue. 8" long, 6 1/2" tall. "Henriot Quimper." c.1930. $650-700.

An assortment of interesting wares.

The artists working in the *faïenceries* of Quimper created some very interesting *jardinières* that may have been made to hold flowers. However these are such exquisite pieces that flowers might distract the eye from the beauty of the item itself.

A *Breton* couple, perhaps courting, adorn this lovely rectangular (with cut corners) *jardinière*. The corners are decorated in a soft geometric pattern. Large gold sponged handles frame this lovely piece. About 14" long, 4" tall. "Henriot Quimper." c.1925. $725-775.

A magnificent piece. Beautifully scalloped rim with raised details above and below the sweet figures. Extravagantly decorated sprays of *ajonc* and *bruyère* frame a sensitively rendered couple visiting over the fence. Whimsical dragon handles in soft yellow and green with vivid blue frame the piece. 8" tall, 15" long. "HR Quimper." c.1910. $1,500-1,700.

Opposite page, bottom: This *jardinière* has all the elements necessary to qualify it as an extraordinary piece! A beautifully rendered dancing couple is featured on the rippled, concave center medallion, which rests on a red striped scallop shell. The exquisite base is bordered in graceful blue and green bands and bears a red criss-cross pattern with blue dots in the squares. The sides of the *jardinière* are painted in a blue and green acanthus *décor* on a pale blue background. Graceful handles in soft yellow and green seem to rise from the sides. 11" tall, 8" wide. "HR Quimper." c.1910. $950-1,000.

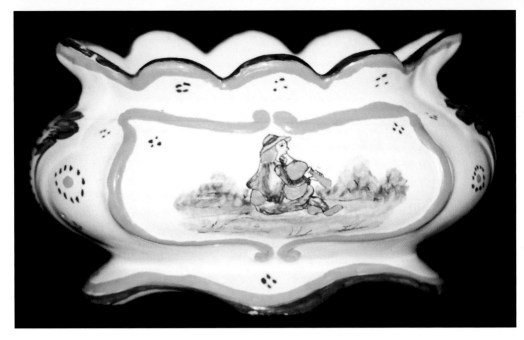

A small *jardinière* with naive *décor*. Lovely scalloped rim and base are banded in blue and gold while the *biniou* player is framed with a gold band and four blue dot *décor*. About 6" long, 3" tall. "Henriot Quimper." c.1935. $450-500.

This sweet little *jardinière* from the *Grande Maison* rests on little feet and features a *petite Bretonne*. About 9" long. "HB Quimper." c.1910. $400-450.

A baby's cradle, complete with rockers for its base. This *Breton* couple rests while on the way to or from the market. She is clad in a blue dress with pink apron, and holds a basket of eggs and a flower while her companion plays a tune for her on the bagpipe. The scene is framed with a blue zig-zag pattern with gold dots. About 10" long, 3.5" tall at corner. "Henriot Quimper." c. 1925. $800-850.

Another version of the same cradle.

A dramatic form. The jardinière features a *Breton* couple topped with a zig-zag rim. It has dragon heads for feet. About 5" tall, 8" long. "HR Quimper." c. 1900. $900-950.

The Henriot factory produced some platters featuring truly remarkable wedding scenes. Each rendering of *La Noce Bretonne* (The *Bretonne* Wedding) is a masterpiece.

As some children watch wide-eyed, a wedding procession led by two musicians passes by. The scene, crowned by the crest of Brittany, is bordered in a rich blue on soft yellow *décor riche* and framed with a deeply scalloped rim. 10.5" x 20". "HR Quimper." c.1910. $2,800-3,000.

Brittany's coat of arms.

Opposite page, bottom: Truly a masterpiece! The rarity and complexity of this scene along with the very large size of the platter account for its value. 15" x 19". "Henriot Quimper." c.1930. $3,600-3,800.

The bride and groom.

Here is another of Alfred Beau's *La Noce Bretonne*, a lovely scene of the wedding party leaving the church. This scene includes even more people and more detail.

The bride and groom.

Two young *Breton* girls in costume, perhaps gazing at a bride and groom.

Faïence copies of wooden shoes and ladies' slippers were perfect little gifts for friends at home or as souvenirs of one's vacation in Brittany.

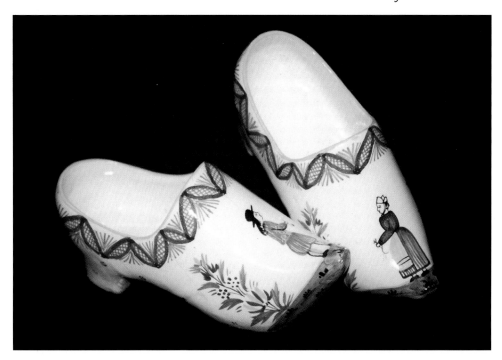

A pair of *sabots* or wooden shoes. Yes, wooden shoes were very popular in Brittany and occasionally today you will see a farmer clad in wooden shoes. This pair features a simply drawn *Breton* couple, flanked by sprays of *a la touche* flowers with blue dot blossoms. Criss-cross and striping details add interest. 8" long. Unmarked. c.1930. $400-450.

A lady's slipper bordered in yellow with a scallop and dot band features a sweet *Bretonne*. It is signed only "HB." About 6" long. c.1900. $350-400.

A slipper-shaped wall pocket. The slipper has a colorful *croisillé* pattern on the back and a blue bow above a *Bretonne*. 8" long. " Henriot Quimper France." c.1925. $425-450.

Another slipper-shaped wall pocket with similar *décor*. 8" long. "Henriot Quimper France." c.1935. $425-450.

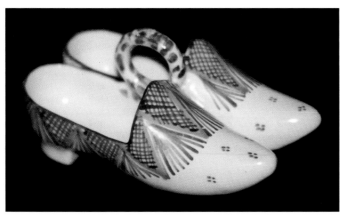

This low-heeled pair of slippers bears a striking *décor* of blue criss-cross, orange stripes, and scattered blue dot *décor*. 4" long. Unsigned, probably "HR." c.1920. $225-250 pr.

A lovely pair of ladies shoes. Blue sponging on the border accentuates the form. *Breton* peasant figures are flanked with orange and blue *touche* blossoms and foliage. 6" long. "HB." c.1910. $350-375 pr.

A dainty high-button shoe poised on a base that reads *Souvenir de Bretagne*. 4" tall. Unsigned but surely from the Porquier factory. c.1905. $325-350.

A very large wooden shoe in the blue *lis* pattern. 10" long, 3" wide. "HB." c.1900. $375-400.

At an antiques show in Paris, I photographed this lovely display of saints and *bénitiers* (holy water fonts). It is a custom in Brittany to give the gift of a little figure of one's patron saint to dear ones.

A very unusual color palette was used on this Ste Anne—all pastels with cobalt and gold trim. 6" tall. "Henriot Quimper." c.1930. $325-350.

Figure of Saint Anne, Mother of *Bretons*, with her child Mary and some kneeling peasants. Molded by Anie Mouroux. 10.5" tall. "Henriot Quimper." Value not available. *Courtesy Musée de la Faïence Quimper.*

Locmaria, where the factory is located is just on the edge of the city of Quimper. Just across the way from the factory stands the ancient church *Notre Dame de Locmaria*. These are some of the treasures to be found in the church:

Sainte Antoine is the patron Saint of *Faïenciers*. Here in the church he holds a baby (presumably the Christ Child) and a Quimper jug. About 5" tall. Value not avaliable.

One of thirteen *faïence* plaques framed in terracotta that were made in the *Grande Maison* in 1859 and 1860 for Notre Dame of Locmaria. About 18" tall. From the HB factory. c.1860. Invaluable!

A lovely baptismal font with Celtic accents.

77

The earliest figures to be produced in the *faïenceries* of Quimper appeared late in the eighteenth century. Most were religious and unmarked. Because France is a predominantly Catholic country, religious wares were very popular and are still highly prized today, along with more secular figures, especially those of *Breton peasants* clad in gaily colored costumes. Often the figures of a particular artist became so popular the artist was asked to sign his wares.

A young *Breton* boy in costume at a Pardon in Locronan. A *Pardon* is a religious celebration, culminating in a procession of pilgrims, with many costumed participants bearing banners and statues.

The serene faces of *Jacques* and *Madalenn* indicate early HR production: he with his *biniou* and she with her basket. 5.25" tall. "HR Quimper." c.1910. $425-450 ea.

Louisik carries her basket to market! She is 5.25" tall. "HR Quimper." c.1910. $425-450.

Marik and *Fanche* have sweet, youthful faces. 5.25" tall. "HR Quimper." c.1910. $425-450 ea.

Sweet little *Bretonne* in a colorful apron and blue striped dress. 4.25" tall. "Henriot Quimper." c.1925. $425-450.

L. H. Nicot is well known for his figures of older *Bretons* and this is a fine example. A *Breton* sits on a rock while saying her rosary. About 10" tall. "Henriot Quimper." Also signed "LH Nicot" on the base. c.1925. $950-1,050.

A classic Nicot figure, an elderly *Bretonne* lady colorfully garbed leans on her cane. 11.25" tall. "Henriot Quimper France." Also signed "LH Nicot" on the base. c.1925. $525-575.

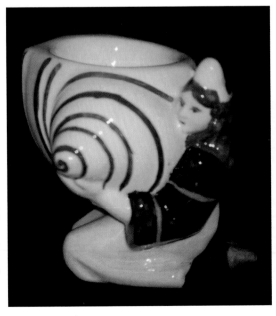

Maillard molded this unique and charming piece. A sweet young lady holding a large conch shell for your egg. 4" tall. "Henriot Quimper Maillard." c.1930. $375-400.

These two plump *Breton* ladies were probably fashioned by Yves Creston, although they are marked only "Henriot Quimper." One figure is vigorously washing her clothes while the other displays her baskets (for salt, pepper, and mustard). Laundress: 5" x 6" (base), 6" tall. Lady with baskets: 7.5" tall, 4.5" (base). c.1925. $675-725 ea.

Serres livres (bookends) sculpted by Berthe Savigny feature the *bébés* for which she is so well known. About 4.5" tall. "HB Quimper." c. 1930. $950-1,000.

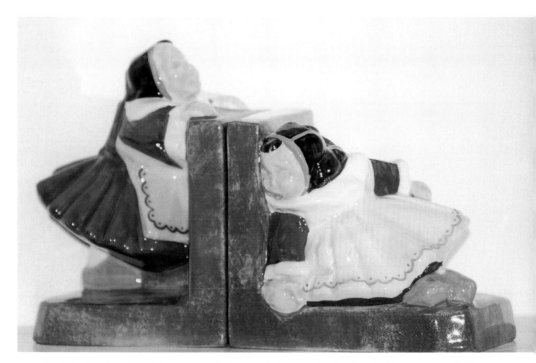

Jim Sévellec fashioned these sweet babies to hold your books. Looks like a game of hide and seek. About 4.5" tall. "Henriot Quimper jes." c. 1910. $950-1,000.

A *Bretonne* in costume for a *Pardon* in Locronan.

André Galland molded this portly *Bretonne* as a mustard pot. A piece from the Modern Movement. 5 1/2" tall. "Henriot Quimper." c.1950. $275-300.

This funny little pelican was probably intended as an ashtray, with a hole in its head for matches. A rare figure. About 5" tall. "HB Quimper." c.1935. $350-375.

A trio of figures, any one of which would add new dimension to a collection. *Left: Loik* carries a sack and a walking stick. 10" tall. "Henriot Quimper." c.1940. $550-600. *Center: A* sweet young *Bretonne*, with her hands in her pockets and bare feet is the creation of Berthe Savigny. 13". "HB Quimper B. Savigny." c.1940. $650-700. *Right:* An Andre Galland figure of a Normand peasant holding a basket. 8" tall. "Normandie AG" 1935. $300-325.

This little lady hides a bell under her skirt. Another Modern Movement figure by André Galland. Her dress is cobalt and her apron is pink. 4" tall. Signed "AG 86 Quimper." c.1935. $275-300.

One of André Galland's most interesting pieces. The happy little *Breton* figure is atop a barrel, perhaps for tobacco. 6" tall. "Henriot Quimper a.g." c.1935. $475-500.

Berthe Savigny's babies are treasured by collectors. This one is clad in a pink dress with scattered blue dot *décor*. 5" tall. "Henriot Quimper." c.1945. $550-600.

This sweet lady holds a basket in her lap. 4" tall. "Henriot Quimper." c.1935. $300-325.

A starched white coiffe frames the pretty face of a young lady. An unusual costume. 6" tall. "Henriot Quimper a.g." c.1935. $375-400.

A very important figure of a young *Breton* by René Quillivic, a fisherman turned sculptor and a celebrated sculptor at that. Titled *Jeune Bigouden* and limited to a production of 200. 19" tall. "HB Quimper Quillivic." c.1925. Value not available. *Courtesy Marie-Thérèse and William Dereure.*

Robert Micheau sculpted *Kemener Kemper,* the tailor of Quimper. Fantastic color! Micheau seems to infuse his figures with life. 7" tall. "Henriot Quimper 145." Before 1930. Value not available. *Courtesy Musée de la Faïence Quimper.*

You will recognize this as another Robert Micheau figure. "The Card Players." 8.5" tall. "Henriot Quimper 145 Robert Micheau." Before 1930. Value not available. *Courtesy Musée de la Faïence Quimper.*

The finished product.

voiter en faïence polychrome

Cette pièce fut réalisée par le modeleur LE
BORGNE et le peintre Pierre ROCUET pour
l'Exposition d'Art Breton qui se tint à QUIMPER
en 1907.
Manufacture HENRIOT
Marque HR QUIMPER

This incredible piece was modeled by Le Borgne and painted by Pierre Rocuet for the 1907 Exposition of *Breton* Art in Quimper. 23.5" tall, 39" long. "HR Quimper." Value not available. *Courtesy Musée de la Faïence Quimper.*

A closer look. Note the concentration on the face of this young *Breton*.

A figure entitled "A Quimper Lady with her Cat" by Georges Robin in *grès*. 10.5" tall. "HB Quimper." c.1930. Value not available. *Courtesy Musée de la Faïence Quimper.*

Snuff bottles, a very popular form at the turn of the nineteenth century, were being produced at all three factories. In most cases they were not signed because their size did not allow space for a signature. Today they are very popular with collectors.

Because there are so many fishing communities in Brittany, we often see wares reflecting the sea. This little fish-shaped snuff is a collector's dream. About 3" long. "Henriot Quimper France." c.1925. $525-575.

A model in *grès* of a potter and his wheel, done sometime after 1950 by Jacques Marie who came to Quimper to create unique wares. 31" tall, 37" long. "Marie." Value not available. *Courtesy Musée de la Faïence Quimper.*

This crest-shaped snuff, produced in the *Grande Maison*, features a primitively rendered *Bretonne*. About 2.5" tall. "HB Quimper." c. 1930. $400-425.

A tiny treasure. A sweet butterfly with wings striped in blue and banded in a soft yellow is just the right size for your pocket. A rare and sought after form. 2" x 3.5". Definitely from Quimper but unsigned. c. 1920. $825-875.

Over the years, inkwells have been produced in a great variety of sizes and shapes. Some of these inkstands were purchased for everyday use and some were undoubtedly purchased strictly for their aesthetic value. Today, inkwells are very sought after by collectors, some of whom collect only Quimper inkwells while others collect inkwells of all kinds.

A little treasure. A very sweet heart-shaped inkwell, nicely painted in a vivid palette. 3" dia. "HB Quimper." c. 1930. $325-350.

A classic symbol of France, the *fleur de lis,* forms this inkwell. Four *fleur de lis* are linked in a square. Inside the tip of each *lis* there is a tiny ermine tail, a symbol of Brittany. 4" tall, 3.5" square. "HR." c. 1900. $425-450.

Criss-cross *décor* accompanied by lots of little stripes and dots decorate three sides of this inkwell. On the fourth side a young *Breton* rests a while with his pipe. Very interesting form. 4" square. "Henriot Quimper." c.1935. $350-375.

Surmounted with a scallop shell and banded in blue stripes, this double inkwell has lost its lids. 6" long. "Henriot Quimper." c.1930. $275-325 (with its lids it would be $525-550).

This is the first boat-shaped inkwell I have seen. I'm sure it had a lid but, as is often the case, it is missing. 6" long. "Henriot Quimper." c.1925. $325-350.

While *Breton* ladies have their lacy coiffes, the men have their broad brimmed, beribboned hats. Interesting combination of geometric and floral *décor* on this inkwell. 6" dia. "HR Quimper." c.1910. $450-475.

Because Brittany enjoys many miles of coastline, life is inexorably tied to the sea. Fishing, an important industry for *Breton*s, has always been a popular theme with the *faïence* artists.

The bagpipe player on this scallop shell is rendered with much more detail than the figure in the photo at left. The floral sprays are typical Henriot *décor*. 8" long, 4.25" wide. "Henriot Quimper France." c.1930. $225-250.

A scallop shell shaped dish produced by the *Grande Maison* HB. Note that the blue blossoms are typical of the *Grande Maison*. 9.25" long, 6" wide. "HB Quimper." c.1930. $225-250.

A *coquille* with a lovely gold bow and cobalt feathering on the rim. 4" dia. "Henriot Quimper France." c.1930. $150 -125.

The wares of Quimper reflect the strong influence of the fishing industry: figures of fishermen and sometimes their womenfolk, boats, sets of dinnerware with a maritime motif, fish-shaped plates, et cetera.

A demure young peasant lady balances a jug, probably of water, on her head. The palette used on this shell is so much more vivid than the shell with bagpipe player on page 92. 7.5" long, 4.5" wide. "Henriot Quimper." c.1930. $250-275.

A sailor mends his basket while sitting on some rocks. A bookend from the Modern Movement period. 6.25" tall, 3" wide. "HB Quimper." c.1930. $300-325.

A *soufflet* (bellows). Porquier Beau production. c.1895. Value not available. *Courtesy Musée de la Fäience Quimper.*

Wall pockets are another favorite with collectors— used for flowers, matches, or simply as decoration.

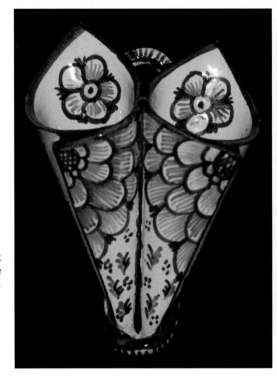

Stylized zinnia blossoms adorn this sweet little double cornet! 4" long. No signature but surely AP. c.1895. $250-275.

A simple little wall cornet featuring a *Bretonne. Petite* blue and orange flowers with four blue dot *décor* scattered about. Tiny and sweet. 4" long. "Henriot Quimper." c.1925. $150-175.

A match holder featuring a man in the costume of Normandy. Criss-cross *décor* with red and green details top it off! 3" tall. "Henriot Quimper." c.1925. $200-225.

This extravagantly decorated pair of *petite* wall pockets, features a peasant couple. Green foliage in relief at the top. 4.5" tall, 2.75" wide. "HR Quimper." c.1910. $500-525.

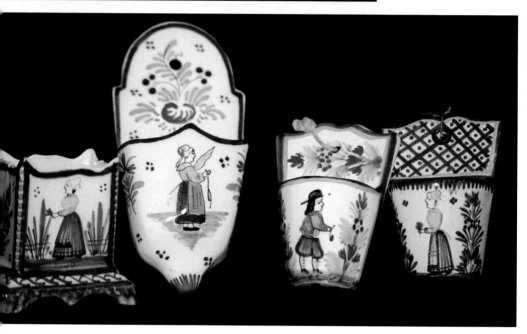

An assortment of little wall pockets and one standing match holder. *From left:* Cobalt blue frames this *Bretonne* with a posey, 4" tall, "HR Quimper." c.1910, $275-300; 5" pocket, unsigned, $175-200; a match holder featuring a *Breton* flanked by sprays of flowers that are repeated across the top, 3" tall, "HR Quimper," c.1910, $200-225; another match holder, this time with a *Bretonne*, topped with blue criss-cross and red dots, 3" tall, "HR Quimper," c.1910, $200-225.

A wonderful form to add to your collection. The envelope-shaped pocket is outlined in cobalt and gold and features a *Breton*. *Demi-fantaisie* sprays decorate each panel. 6.25" x 6.25". "HR Quimper." c.1910. $450-475.

Cornucopia shaped wall pocket decorated with yellow *ajonc* and pink *bruyère* blossoms. A very dapper young *Breton* relaxes by the fence. 10" long, 6.25" wide. "Henriot Quimper." c.1925. $525-550.

Both the form and *décor* on this triple pocket are superb. The piece features a dapper young man from Normandy on his way to market. Tall floral sprays frame the figure. Blue criss-cross decorates the back panel. 6" tall, 6" wide. Signed only "Lisieux," but surely from the Henriot factory. c.1925. $375-425.

This *parapluie* (umbrella) wall pocket was probably never meant to hold anything as it is quite lovely on its own. Both the form and *décor* are exquisite. The ubiquitous pair of *Breton* musicians, one playing the *bombarde*, the other the *biniou*, are seen strolling the countryside. Vivid blue on blue *décor riche* border and rippled form. 14" long, 9" wide. "Henriot Quimper." c.1925. $700-750.

Very early vase meant to be hung with a ribbon through the loops on the sides. A finely rendered *Breton* with one hand in his pocket. Interesting blue on blue geometric trim. About 7" x 6". Signed only "HB." c.1895. $600-650.

The *Musée des Beaux-Arts de Quimper* has a fabulous collection of large paintings that depict *Breton* life. My special favorite is a painting entitled *Les Jouers des Boules* by Théophile Déyrolle (1844-1893), a highly regarded *Breton* artist. Some of Déyrolle's scenes were painted on *faïence* by Alfred Beau while he was employed at the Porquier factory. Others were re-created by Paul Fouillen at the HB factory, and some by the Henriot factory. The example below was produced by the Henriot factory.

Looks like a serious game of *boules*. All eyes are focused on the player with the ball. The scene is encircled by a wide border *décor* of sprays of yellow *ajonc*. About 18" dia. "*d'apres* Deyrolle Henriot Quimper." c.1930. $2,400-2,600.

A masterpiece!

A steaming cup of hot coffee or tea is just right on a cold, damp winter morning in Brittany. As the *faïenceries* provided for the needs of every *Breton* kitchen, tea pots and coffee pots were produced in a myriad of shapes and patterns. The examples pictured here represent only a few of the many different forms and *décors* of coffee and tea pots produced in the very prolific period between the two world wars.

This ensemble of jug, coffee pot, and sugar bowl look wonderful on this tray. These are all wares from the HB factory. The *décor* is distinctively theirs. The tray features a bagpipe player and a horn player bordered by alternating panels of criss-cross and stylized sprays of *ajonc*. The other pieces feature finely drawn peasants, soft background detail, and floral sprays. All are signed "HB Quimper." All c. 1935. Sugar bowl (4" tall) and teapot (8" tall): $450-500. Jug (12" tall): $375-400. Tray (13.5" x 16.5"): $750-800.

Fantastic rippled form. The pot features *demi-fantaisie décor*, scattered blue dot flowers, and scallop and dot bands. Wonderful handle, spout, and finial frame a sweet *Bretonne*. 11" tall. "Henriot Quimper." c. 1925. $650-700.

Tête à tête. A great find—the complete set, including the tray. Classic *demi fantaisie décor*. Pot: 7" tall, 9" wide. Sugar: 4" tall, 4.5" wide. Creamer: 3" tall, 6" wide. "Hennriot Quimper France." c.1935. $l,400-1,600.

This teapot features classic HB *decor*. Note the *décor* so you can identify this pattern as HB even when unsigned. Very interesting form with cut corners and red criss-cross. 7.5" tall. "HB Quimper." c.1935. $375-400.

A group of *Breton*s at a *Pardon* (a religious procession).

Wonderful, large coffee pot. *Breton Broderie décor.* 10" tall. "HB Quimper." c. 1930. $425-450.

Tea for two in very sweet *décor*. Rounded forms are decorated in a soft palette of yellow, pale blue, and red. Portly *Breton* featured on the teapot. Large two handled tray. Tray is about 14" dia. "Henriot Quimper." c.1930. $1100-1200.

This generous coffee pot with a bulbous base is gently squared off, decorated with tall *demi-fantaisie* sprays, and a sweeping handle bordered in gold and striped in blue. 9.5" tall, 9.5" wide. "Henriot Quimper France." c.1925. $650-700.

Six-lobed teapot and creamer in the "oh so French" *décor* of *fleur de lis* and ermine tails. Wares are bordered with blue chain, while handles and spout are striped in blue. Pot is 6.5" tall. "HB." c.1900. $725-750.

When the French set a table, they have everything you might want or need, even an object on which to rest your knife when not using it. You certainly wouldn't want to soil the tablecloth by placing your knife on it. Here are a few examples of knife rests from the Quimper factories.

An amusing (and rare) pair of figural knife rests made for the Henriot factory. 3.75" long. "HR Quimper." c.1920. $275-300 ea.

Four colorful, figural knife rests made by Charles Maillard in the Modern Movement years (1920s and 30s). 4.5" and 5" long. "Henriot Quimper c.m." c.1935. $200-225 ea.

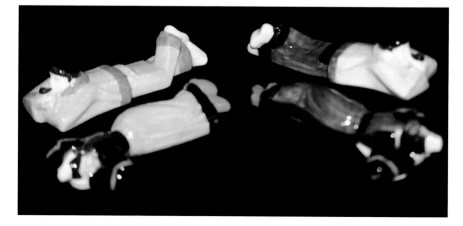

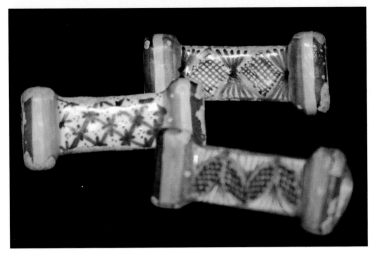

Three nineteenth-century knife rests decorated with interesting geometric *décors* in vivid blue, orange, green, and yellow. There is considerable wear on the ends of each piece. 2.5" long. Surely from Quimper but which factory? c.1890. $60 ea.

Many years ago, in Brittany, baby bottles were shaped like those in the following photos. They were quite small with a spout like the one seen on the far left. This assortment, of various sizes, today would be used for cider or water. The two on the right are from the HB factory and the two on the left are from the Henriot *faïencerie*. Pitchers of all sizes and shapes were produced in a plethora of patterns and are always popular with collectors.

A *biberon* with its cover. Wonderful big blossoms and blue striped handles with scattered blue dot *décor*. 10" tall. "Henriot Quimper." c.1930. $425-450.

An early naive *cruche* with four handles. 7" tall. "HB Quimper." c. 1925. $450-475.

What an interesting form. Created by C. Maillard, whose work was very well received in the 1920s and 30s. Production of Maillard's work continued into the 1950s. 8" tall. "Henriot Quimper c.m." c. 1935. $450-475.

An assortment of biberons.

A pair of pedestal base pitchers for cider. One features a naively rendered *Bretonne* and the other a bouquet of stylized blossoms. Both about 8" tall. Both "Henriot Quimper." Both c.1930. $425-450 ea.

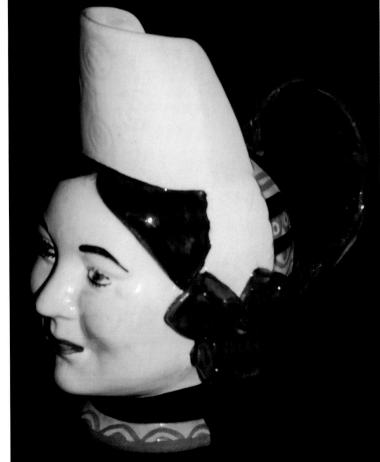

One might expect this *Bretonne* to speak at any moment, she is so life-like. Molded by C. Maillard. 6.75". "Henriot Quimper c.m." c.1935. $450-500.

Wonderful form with a demure lady in the medallion. Gold sponged handle, rim, and base. Floral sprays in gold, blue, and green. About 10" tall. "Henriot Quimper France." c.1930. $475-500.

take a "grand tour" of Europe. Often the grand tour included a visit to the *faïenceries* in Quimper. Many Americans fell in love with the brightly colored pottery and brought home two or three choice pieces—perhaps a little tea set, candlesticks, a *biberon*, or a *jardinière*. The *"Petit Breton"* figure captivated the hearts and imaginations of many.

During the first half of the twentieth century, especially between the two world wars, the wares being produced in the HB and Henriot factories enjoyed a period of enormous popularity. Both factories produced tablewares and accessories for the consumer market in Brittany and France, as well as interesting objects for the many tourists visiting Brittany and for the expanding market in the United States.

After World War I, it was considered very fashionable in America to

A sweet maiden resting with a basket of eggs at her side. *Croisillé décor* with interesting geometric shapes combines with the figure on this lovely candlestick. More than likely, the other candlestick was broken and discarded. 8" tall. "HR Quimper." c.1910. $375-400.

Many of today's collectors remember beginning a collection because of a single piece given to them by their grandmother or recall with fondness, "I was brought up with Quimper ware, we used it every day." Any of the following pieces could have been the first piece of what would become a large collection.

Beautifully crafted and decorated, this chamberstick is a treasure. About 4" square. "Henriot Quimper France." c.1925. $400-425.

A pair of candlesticks, a form so sought after. Though not as old as you might wish, a pair none the less. The *Breton* couple is accented with typical orange and green touche flowers with blue and yellow dot blossoms. 8" tall. "Henriot Quimper BHV" (BHV is the name of a department store in Paris). c.1950. $425-450.

A candlestick in the *Pyrenées décor* features a lady clad in the local style. 10" tall. Signed only "Alsace" but surely from HB. c.1930. $275-300.

An outstanding example of artistry from the Henriot factory. The egg server will hold six egg cups and six eggs. The blue rim, blue *fleur de lis,* and large, graceful blue handle enhance the piece. 5" tall, 11" dia. "HR Quimper." c.1910. $675-700.

A giant mug for your morning coffee features a *Petit Breton* and tall sprays of blue and orange blossoms with green foliage and scattered blue dot *décor*. 5" tall. "Henriot Quimper." c.1925. $200-225.

A little treasure, easy to tuck into your suitcase and bring home! This tiny easel holds a typical *Petit Breton* plate. 4.75" tall, 3" dia. Unsigned. c.1910. $300-325.

A Rococo style menu with a raised border in blue and gold features a finely rendered lady holding a distaff. 6.75" tall, 5.25" wide. "HR Quimper." $450-475.

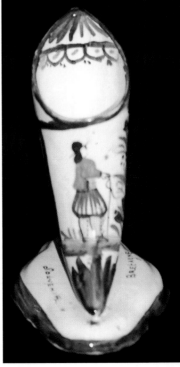

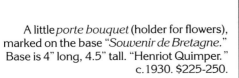

A little *porte bouquet* (holder for flowers), marked on the base "*Souvenir de Bretagne.*" Base is 4" long, 4.5" tall. "Henriot Quimper." c. 1930. $225-250.

An assortment of wares to tempt a visitor to Brittany.

A pair of door plaques that will keep your memories of Brittany fresh. About 9" long. "HB Quimper." c. 1930. $625-650.

In the first half of the eighteenth century, the French government suffered a financial crisis resulting in a mandate for the confiscation of all precious metals. Since tablewares were often made of precious metals, there was suddenly a need for a substitute. *Voila!* The *faïenceries* of Quimper stepped up production. Plates were decorated with colorful geometric patterns, and primitive figures as well as detailed figures! Over the years, many more patterns have been added.

Geometric *décors* were produced in the nineteenth century and well into the 1960s. They have always been very popular, surely due to their vivid colors and imaginative design. 9.5" dia. "HB Quimper." c.1925. $400-425 ea.

The *demi-fantaisie décor*, that is, sprays of orange *a la touche* and blue dot blossoms with green *touche* foliage decorate this pair of plates. 10.5" dia. "Henriot Quimper France." c.1935. $600-700 pr.

The same *demi-fantaisie décor* as in the photo on bottom of page 112, but this pair is older and many details have been added. Wonderful scalloped rim. 10.5" dia. "Henriot Quimper." c.1925. $725-750 pr.

Another deeply scalloped plate but here, the blue on blue *décor riche* border frames the figure of a young man. 10.5" dia. "Henriot Quimper." c.1950. $425-450.

Still another pair. Rich *croisillé décor* alternating with stylized blossoms, interesting chain band encircles the finely drawn figures. Remember, this *croisillé* pattern is from the Henriot factory. 10.5" dia. "Henriot Quimper." c.1925. $775-800 pr.

A two-toned blue *fleur de lis*, the symbol of France, is featured here. Simple but exquisite. 10" dia. "HB." c.1900. $375-400.

The floral sprays on this plate are from the HB factory. Look for them on other HB wares also, and soon you will know the manufacturer because you recognize the florals as the work of the *Grande Maison*. 9.5" dia. "HB Quimper." c.1925. $325-350.

Here you see the same florals as in the above photo, but now they alternate with blue *croisillé* panels. This is the *Grande Maison*'s version of the *croisillé décor*. Beautifully rendered *Breton* couple! 9.5" dia. "HB Quimper." c.1925. $850-900.

Another from the *Grande Maison* but this time, note the *croisillé* is red with a little blue added. Soup bowl, 10" dia. "HB Quimper." c.1925. $425-450.

Rare border *dècor* on this plate that features an exquisitely rendered *Breton*. This rather serious gent is playing the *"bombarde"* (horn), not a *"biniou"* as noted below the figure. 9" dia. "HB." c.1900. $350-375.

Ajonc (yellow gorse) and *Bruyère* (heather) are featured on the border of this charming plate. A gold band and cobalt scalloped band. 9.5" dia. "Henriot Quimper. c.1925. $400-425.

Same *décor* as in the above photo but here featuring a young *Breton* couple. Vivid palette. 9.5". "Henriot Quimper." c.1925. $475-500.

This very popular genre is from the HB factory and always features a nicely rendered figure, thus the pattern name "naive yet detailed." *A la touche* foliage sprays alternate with blue dot *décor* on the border and flank the dapper gent. Take note of the uneven, thin glaze on the border—often indicative of early wares. 9 1/2" dia. "HB." c.1895. $400-425.

Just when you think you have seen everything, something unique appears. Believe it or not this is a close-up of the *décor* on a 9.5" dia. plate. "*Automobile juin 1927 Germaine Rochette no34/18 HenRiot Quimper Edité par la Crémaillère.*" 1927. Value not available. *Courtesy Musée de la Faïence Quimper.*

Chapter Seven
Paul Fouillen and Odetta

Paul Fouillen trained at the Beaux Arts School in Rennes and began his career as a decorator in the *Grande Maison* in 1920. Early in his tenure, he designed the *Pecheur* pattern, characterized by a shell and seaweed border, a fisherman and his lady in the foreground, and a geometric rendering of the landscape in the background. A series of port scenes, in a more realistic style, followed. Portraits were a popular subject for *Monsieur* Fouillen and they were sometimes carved and painted on wood.

In 1924, Fouillen became the director of the three decorating studios at the *Grande Maison,* while continuing to design and decorate *faïence and wood.* In 1925, Fouillen began molding and painting *grès* for a new line of wares called Odetta. Odetta wares are characterized by angular lines and vivid colors. The Odetta line was a great success and remained in production until 1960.

In 1929, Fouillen opened his own factory very near the site of the HB factory. Wares from his own factory were simply marked "PFouillen."

All of Fouillen's work, which often reflects the Celtic heritage of Brittany, was very popular. Today the wares he produced while at the *Grande Maison* can be easily recognized because they were signed "PFouillen HB Quimper. "

This *panier* is full of pieces from the Modern Movement, all but one (vase second from right by Sevellec) are the work of Paul Fouillen. 1915 to 1950.

Many of Fouillen' figures are very angular and ofte the background blocks of stone a you see on this cake plate and server. Plate is 9" dia. and server is 10" long. Both signed "PFouillen." c.1935. $650-700.

A wonderful piece. The body of the pitcher is banded with typical Celtic decor. A unique handle in the shape of a *Bretonne*. Fouillen made several jugs with figural handles, both *Bretons* and *Bretonnes*. 6" tall. "PFouillen Quimper." c.1930. $350-375.

A little biberon with all the characteristics of Paul Fouillen's style. Portrait of a *Bretonne* with her head tilted down, blocks of stone in the background, and a red Celtic inspired scroll. About 6" tall. "P Fouillen." c.1935. $125-150.

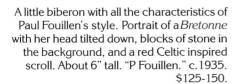

Monsieur Fouillen's wooden wares often featured angular portraits and stone blocks, as seen here in a portrait of a *Bretonne*. Approx. 10". "PFouillen." c.1935. $325-375.

These door plaques are signed only "HBQuimper" but are surely the work of Fouillen. The *Bretonne* lady stands atop a megalith, while the musicians play the *biniou* and *bombarde*. Rare and wonderful. 2" wide, 8.5" long. "HB Quimper." c.1925. $850-900.

A wonderful *Breton* couple. Each one is artfully drawn in Fouillen's angular style. Note their expressive faces. A wooden cut-out. About 10" long. "PFouillen." c.1935. $300-325.

The year 1999 marks the 100th anniversary of the birth of Paul Fouillen. On a visit to Quimper in July 1999, I visited the Fouillen factory just around the corner from the HB-Henriot factory. Many exciting pieces made by Fouillen were on display. Although conditions for taking photographs were limited, I share with you these fantastic wares.

An array of figures including *Tintin,* a character from French children's literature. *Courtesy of Maurice Fouillen.*

A closer look at *Tintin.* About 4" tall. *Courtesy of Maurice Fouillen.*

An incredible Modern Movement style Ste. Anne. *Courtesy of Maurice Fouillen.*

And another *Courtesy of Maurice Fouillen.*

A phantasmagorical creature. *Courtesy of Maurice Fouillen.*

Jug and matching cup with a maritime motif. *Courtesy of Maurice Fouillen.*

Vase about 10" tall. *Courtesy of Maurice Fouillen.*

Portrait plate of a *Breton*. 10" dia. *Courtesy of Maurice Fouillen.*

A *Bretonne. Courtesy of Maurice Fouillen.*

Striking vase in a dramatic color palette and bold geometric shapes. Portrait of a *Breton. Courtesy of Maurice Fouillen.*

A very exciting piece. The blue is electric!
Courtesy of Maurice Fouillen.

Enchanting picture painted on wood. Note the Quimper cup.
Courtesy of Maurice Fouillen.

The back of a chair carved and painted by PFouillen. *Courtesy of Maurice Fouillen.*

A trio of *Bretonnes* in a circle. Painted on wood. About 7" tall. *Courtesy of Maurice Fouillen.*

A few modern movement pieces.

A vase by René Olichon. Rich cobalt blue. 10" tall. "HB Quimper ROL 602 1320." 602 is the form and 1320 refers to the *décor.* c.1930. Value not available. *Courtesy Musée de la Faïence Quimper.*

A vase by René Beauclair with geometric *décor*. About 10" tall. "HB Quimper René Beauclair 673 1352." c.1930. Value not available. *Courtesy Musée de la Faïence Quimper.*

Pitcher featuring a portrait of a *Breton* in a central medallion. Intense palette of color. "HB Quimper Odetta 295." 4" tall. c.1930. $750-800.

A final *mélange* of wares from the Quimper *faïenceries*.

A sweet little yellow double salt. A pair of hearts featuring a *Breton* couple. 5" long. "Henriot Quimper France." c. 1930. $140-160. Carved wooden *Breton* doll's chair. 8" tall. $150-165.

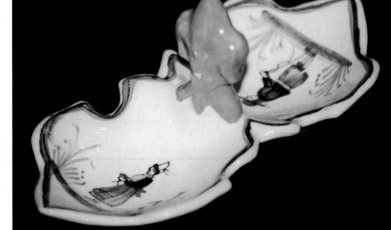

Fleur de lis handle joins two little bowls for salt. 5" long. "Henriot Quimper." c. 1930. $150-165.

The border on this plate is quite unusual. Cobalt acanthus leaf border with scallop shells at top and bottom frame a demure *Bretonne* who is spinning wool. Beautifully rendered figure and background. 10". "HB Quimper." c.1925. $500-550.

An incredible picture frame in Rococo *décor* with lovely floral sprays and an exquisitely rendered *Breton* couple. "HR." c.1910. Value not available. *Courtesy Musée de la Faïence Quimper.*

Figure of a handsome, older *Breton* with his arms folded. Beautifully molded and painted. 9" tall. "HB Quimper." c.1930. $525-550.

One of a 3 part series of framed, sculpted plaques set in the Congo. Scene of a woman offering a drink to a man as a percussionist looks on. 16" x 18". Sculpted by Émile Monier for "Henriot Quimper." c.1935. Value not available. *Courtesy of Musée de la Faïence Quimper.*

An incredible piece. A castle in three pieces sculpted in 1877. Cover lifts off to reveal a basin for water. Note the two spigots near the base. It is rare for a nineteenth-century piece to be signed by the artist. About 20" tall, 16" wide. *"A Masson fecit 1877 HB."* Value not available. *Courtesy Musée de la Faïence Quimper.*

Pièce unique. Lovely rendition of man holding two platters of fresh strawberries. Wonderful rippled border of berries. Scalloped rim is banded in blue. 10" dia. "HB Quimper." c. 1930. $375-400.

A trio of dolls bowls in wonderful blue, yellow, orange, and green. *Left:* 3.5" dia., "Henriot Quimper," c.1930. *Center:* 2.5" dia., "HR Quimper," c.1910. *Right:* 3" dia., "HR Quimper," c.1910. $100-125 ea.

Sweet little doll's bowl banded in cobalt with tiny orange *touches* and green dots. 2" dia., 1.5" tall. "HR Quimper." c.1910. $100-125.

Pair of bowls for your dolls decorated with brightly colored *touches* and banded in blue and yellow. 3" dia. "Henriot Quimper." c.1925. $75-90.

134

A menu card in a graceful crest form, chain border, the crest of Brittany featuring a dapper *Breton* in his puffy pants and broad brimmed hat. 5" x 6.5". "HB." c.1900. $600-650.

Soupière in classic Quimper *décor*. Features a *Breton* couple, tall *arbustes* (floral sprays) of blue and orange *touche* blossoms with scattered blue dot *décor*. 7" tall, 8" dia. (lid). "HR Quimper." c.1910. $675-700.

An extravagantly decorated *broderie* plate accented with raised (*au poire*) white dots and Celtic swirls. 9.25" dia. "HB Quimper." c.1935. $350-375.

An exquisite covered butter dish. Octagonal shape, rippled cover and plate, delicate *demi-fantaisie décor,* scattered ermine tails, *petit Breton* and interesting finial—what more could you want? Base: 9.5" dia. "HR Quimper." c.1910. $525-550.

Classic Fouillen *décor* featuring a *Breton* on a bulbous vase. "Pfouillen." About 4" dia. c.1930. $275-300.

Fantastic pair of plaques in relief. The border, because it is raised, appears to frame the subjects. Interesting figures with sweet faces and finely rendered gaily colored clothing. 11" long, 7" wide. Unmarked but surely early "HB." Look in my first book on page 11 for another example that is signed with the first "HB" mark. c.1870. $2,400 pr.

Our young *Breton* relaxes with his pipe. Clad in the traditional manner. About 11" tall. "PB Quimper." c.1925. $1,000-1,100.

This is the sweetest covered trinket box from the Quimper factories that I have seen. Richly decorated in blue on blue *décor riche*, the heart features a young *Breton* probably playing a Celtic tune. 5" wide. "Henriot Quimper." c.1925. $450-475.

An exquisite inkwell lavishly decorated in blue and yellow acanthus *décor* in relief. Even the ink pots and lids are beautifully molded. Lions and crests in the center are framed by blue crisscross with red dots. Little blue striped feet underneath. About 14" long. "HR Quimper." c. 1910. $3,000.

The *décor* on this oval plate is classic Quimper. Begin with a simply rendered *Breton* framed with tall à la touche florals. The plate is rimmed in blue with a border of red and green touches alternating with blue dots. Four blue dot *décor* above the figure. About 8" long. "HR Quimper." $325-350

A trio of *Breton* figures including a bagpipe player and a *bombarde* player garbed in the traditional *bragoubraz* (puffy pants) with blue jackets and vests. Marik is perhaps sewing. *From left:* "Youenn," about 4.5" tall, "Henriot Quimper," c.1930, $275-300. "Marik," about 4" tall, "Henriot Quimper," c.1930, $275-300. "Colaik," about 3" tall, "Henriot Quimper," c.1935, $200-225.

An early charger featuring a primitively rendered *Breton* surrounded by classic early *à la touche* décor of green, orange, and blue. Center panel is encircled with one yellow and two black bands, typical of early wares. 10" dia. Unsigned. c.1890, $450-500.

Almost a match to the photo on bottom of page 140. The rough spots on the rim do not affect the price of this nineteenth-century piece—it is old after all. 10" dia. Unsigned. c. 1890. $450-500.

Three pieces decorated in the Henriot *croissilé décor* that is so popular with collectors. A small, oval, handled bowl for bonbons. About 8" long, "Henriot Quimper," c. 1930, $350-400. *Lower left:* A covered trinket box. About 4" dia., c. 1930, $275-300. *Lower right:* A sweet Quintal featuring a *Breton* with his *bombarde*. About 5" dia., "Henriot Quimper," c. 1930, $225-250.

Did the *Mayflower* really sail into Plymouth harbor flying the French flag? I think not! Certainly a patriotic rendition of a souvenir piece in red, white, and blue. 9.5". Unsigned but surely from Henriot. c. 1925. $600-650.

Three variations of the *Ivoire Corbeille* pattern. *Left and right:* 8"; *center:* 9". All signed "Henriot Quimper." c. 1935. $250-275 ea.

A double inkwell decorated with great attention to detail. Blue criss-cross with red dots on the top and wells ringed with a red chain. A sweet *Bretonne* holding a posey and flanked by two delicately rendered floral sprays. A souvenir of *St. Gildas-des-Bois*. About 5" long. Unsigned, probably AP. c.1910. $575-625.

A sweet little pocket for matches featuring a tiny *Breton*. Decorated with orange and green *touches* and blue dot *décor*. About 4" wide. "HB Quimper." c.1930. $225-250.

An *Ivoire Corbeille* rendition of the popular fish shaped plate. This is a very popular rendition because it is so amusing. About 9" dia. "Henriot Quimper." c.1935. $250-275.

An exquisite *Breton* scene by Alfred Beau, made by the Henriot factory after they purchased the Porquier marks and patterns. About 10" x 16". "PB Quimper." c.1920. $2,000-2,100.

Geometrics are quite popular with collectors because the colors are the traditional Quimper colors and they are so very bright and sunny. *Left:* 9.5" stylized flower featuring blue criss-cross with bright yellow, orange, and green accents. "Henriot Quimper." c.1930. $300-325. *Right:* 8" plate with orange criss-cross, bright yellow, blue, and green. "Henriot Quimper." c.1925. $300-325.

A marvelous *parapluie* (umbrella) to hang on the wall. This is the sweetest one I have seen. Soft blue bow striped in cobalt. The umbrella has a deeply scalloped rim with a delicate band of tiny blue dots with little blossoms. A finely rendered *Bretonne* carries a water jug. Exquisite! About 10" long. "HB Quimper." c.1925. $900-950.

A sweet, primitively rendered little plat featuring a *Breton* couple flanked with floral sprays. Border *décor* of orange, green, and blue with cut corners with black ermine tails. A little piece. About 4" x 6". "Henriot Quimper." c.1924. $300-325.

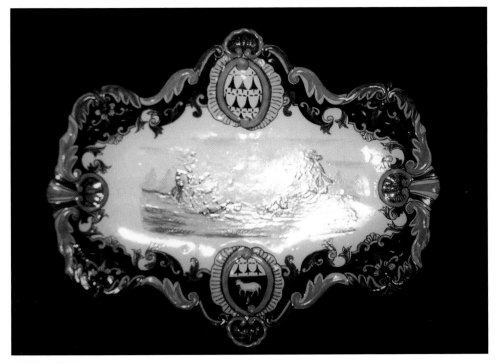

A Rococo style plate featuring a sweet *Breton* couple. Ornate *décor* in relief in blue, gold, and green. About 8" x 12". "HR Quimper." c.1910. $650-700.

Chapter Eight
Faux Faïence

Malicorne is located east of Quimper, near Le Mans, in central France. Late in the nineteenth century, Leon Pouplard, owner of Malicorne's *Pouplard-Béatrix* factory (established in 1750), must have paid a visit to Quimper, because many of his wares feature scenes of *Breton* peasants, which were so characteristic of the *faïence of* Quimper. As a matter of fact, in many instances, the figures and scenes are exact copies. *Monsieur* Pouplard also began marking his wares "PB," which resulted in a lawsuit filed by the Porquier factory. The lawsuit claimed that Pouplard's use of the "PB" mark was an infringement on their "PB" mark. The Porquier factory prevailed. Pouplard scratched off the mark from his existing inventory and continued production, often not marking his newer wares at all, using "PBx" when he did mark his wares.

Until recently most Quimper collectors were uninterested in the wares from Malicorne; however this has changed. Many collectors now mix their Quimper with Malicorne, and some are concentrating exclusively on wares from Malicorne. While Pouplard produced "copies" of Quimper ware, today these pieces stand on their own.

The wares from Malicorne have several distinguishing characteristics: a coarse red clay was used, the painting was done with a finer line, the faces are more often sweet, and the thin glaze allows a pinkish tone to come through.

Desvres (pronounced Dev - re) is located in the most northern part of France, in Normandy. In the eighteenth century, there were two factories in Desvres, and, in 1827, a third appeared. The Fourmaintraux families were the region's principal potters. They produced wares in various Rouen *décors* and, during the late nineteenth and early twentieth century, turned out wares in the *Petit Breton* style. Several pieces are pictured here; however, regretfully, I am unable to show the marks for these pieces as I did not keep a record of them.

The following wares are from the Malicorne and Desvres factories.

Malicorne platter featuring a sweet *Breton* family, including the dog. Unsigned, but surely Malicorne. 11" x 15.5". Unsigned. Malicorne. c.1900. $650-700.

A simple, yet charming plate featuring a peasant strolling along a country path. 8.5" dia. "PBx." c.1900. $250-275.

Fantastic form—a lyre. Delicately rendered figures and flowers. To be hung on the wall. About 8" long, 6" wide. Unsigned, but surely Malicorne. c. 1900. $650-700.

Pair of plates in the traditional Quimper style but from Malicorne. 9.5". "PBx." c. 1900. $250-275 pr.

Cornet with a ruffled rim to hang on the wall. Attractive *fleur de lis* and ermine tail *décor* with a young *Breton* playing the *biniou* (bagpipe). About 10" long. Unsigned, but surely Malicorne. c.1900. $400-425.

A Malicorne vase with dramatic light blue handles dotted in cobalt. A young man from "Guincamp" against a background of evergreen trees. Little sprays of *ajonc* on each side of the figure. About 8" tall. "PBx." c.1900. $250-275.

Pair of Malicorne plates in the colorful leaf and nut border. Finely rendered charming figures. 9.5" dia. "PBx." c.1900. $650-700 pr.

Another pair. Note that the *Breton* carries live fowl in his baskets. 9.5" dia. Unsigned but surely Malicorne. c.1900. $650-700 pr.

A bagpipe wall pocket featuring a courting couple. Pink bow sits atop the bagpipe. About 6" long. "PBx." c.1900. $275-300.

A charming little vase with snake handles. Demure *Breton* with a distaff. Blue on blue acanthus *décor* on the sides and a *fleur de lis* on the reverse. 4.25" tall. Unsigned, but surely Malicorne. c.1900. 350-375.

Wonderful *pitché* banded in blue and featuring two-toned blue *fleur de lis*. 6" tall. "PBx." c.1900. $275-300.

Very interesting form—a crescent with arching handles and pedestal base. 6" tall. "PBx." c.1900. $750-800 pr.

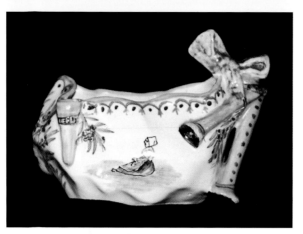

A very unique form—delicate bagpipe shaped *poche* (holder) with dainty floral sprays, scallop and dot border, and pink bow. 4.5" long, 2" tall. Unsigned, but surely Malicorne. c.1900. $225-250.

An exquisite Malicorne handled bowl. Wonderful green on pale blue *décor riche* border featuring a marvelous scene of a *Breton* knife sharpener at work while two boys rough house. Finely drawn with great attention to detail. About 14" from handle to handle. "PBx." c.1900. $900-1,000.

Delicate blue on blue border frames a *Breton* with his walking stick. Lovely scalloped rim. 11" x 15". "PBx." c.1900. $650.

An octagonal plate with blue on yellow *décor riche* border, featuring a dapper young *Breton* with his walking stick. 8.5" dia. Signature unknown but surely Desvres. c.1925. $450-500.

An exquisite Desvres clock with many details in relief including a *Breton* couple. Note the raised details on the side. Magnificent. About 12" tall. Signature unknown but certainly Desvres. c. 1900. $3,800.

An adorable little *jardinière*. A *Bretonne* rests on her way to market. Delicate background and sweet sprays of *bruyère* (heather). 8" long, 6" wide. Signature unknown but surely from Desvres. c. 1910. $350-375.

A sweet double wall pocket featuring a couple from Normandy. "Deauville" on the front indicates that the piece would be sold in Deauville probably as a souvenir. About 5" long. Signature unknown but surely from Desvres. c.1910. $250-300.

Chapter Nine

Major Events in the History of the Faïenceries of Quimper

16 0—Jean Baptiste Bousquet establishes the first *faïencerie* in Quimper, to be known as the *Grande Maison HB*.

1⁷ '9—François Eloury opens a *faïencerie* in Locmaria, to be known later as the Eloury-Porquier factory and still later as the Porquier factory.

1 89—Guillaume Dumaine opens a factory in Quimper for the production of *grès*, known later as the Henriot factory.

369—The first marks appear: HB, AP, HR.

872—Alfred Beau is hired by the Porquier factory.

875—A partnership is formed between Madame Porquier and Alfred Beau.

1882—First HB mark is registered.

1883—Second HB mark is registered.

1893—Alfred Beau leaves the PB factory.

1898—The marks AP and two versions of PB are registered.

1903—The Porquier Beau factory closes; however the inventory is gradually sold off using the AP mark.

1904—The word "Quimper" is thought to have been added consistently to all marks, although it had been used well before 1904 (probably when factories in other parts of France began producing very similar wares).

1913—Jules Henriot purchases the *aquarelles*, molds, and *poncifs* of the Porquier factory.

1917—Jules Verlingue becomes the sole owner of the *Grande Maison*.

1919—The Henriot factory reissues Porquier-Beau wares with the mark "PB Quimper."

1922—The "HR" mark of the Henriot factory is changed to "HenRiot" following a lawsuit by the *Grande Maison HB*.

1968—*Grande Maison HB* purchases the marks and models of the Henriot factory (all three factories are one), known then as *Les Faïenceries de Quimper*. "F" was added to the marks with a number for form, and "d" was added with a number for *décor*, usually written in black.

1983—*Les Faïenceries de Quimper* files for bankruptcy.

1984—*Les Faïenceries de Quimper* is purchased by a group of Americans led by Sarah and Paul Janssens.

1990—*Les Faïenceries de Quimper* purchases the Keraluc factory (located in Quimper).

Bibliography

Bondhus, Sandra V. *Quimper Pottery: A French Folk Art Faïence.* N. p.,
. 1981.

Datesman, Joan. *Collecting Quimper, Quimper Collections.* N. p., n. d.

Graviano, Tony. *The Old Quimper Review* 6, no. 2 (October 1995).

Mali, Millicent S. *French Faïence: Fantasie et Populaire of the 19th and
20th Centuries.* N. p.: United Printing, 1986.

Meadows, Adela. *Quimper Pottery: A Guide to its Origins, Styles, and
Value.* Atglen, Pennsylvania: Schiffer Publishing Ltd., 1998.

Musée des Beaux-Arts, Quimper. *Trois Siécles de Faïences 1690—1990
Catalogue, Editions Ouèst France, Ville de Quimper,* 1990.

Roullot, Michel J. *Les Faïences Artistiques de Quimper aux XVIII et XIX
Siècles.* Lorient, Art-Média, 1980.